of failure & faith

# of failure and faith

poems by

d. ellis phelps

© 2023 d. ellis phelps. All rights reserved.
This material may not be reproduced in any form, published,
reprinted, recorded, performed, broadcast,
rewritten, or redistributed without
the explicit permission of d. ellis phelps.
All such actions are strictly prohibited by law.

Cover image *repurposed wall* by d. ellis phelps

ISBN: 978-1-63980-301-9

Kelsay Books
502 South 1040 East, A-119
American Fork, Utah 84003
Kelsaybooks.com

for my husband

acknowledgments

gratitude to the publications where these poems first appeared in supporting the publication of my poetry:

Amethyst Review: "mama i want to tell you," "rachmaninoff off key"
Animal Tales Anthology: "birdspeak," "washing my breakfast cup"
Boundless Anthology: "maybe i can," "mouth of madness"
Enchantment of the Ordinary Anthology: "birdfeeder"
The Larger Geometry Anthology: "shape   a prayer"
New Texas: "homilies of spring," "limestone blessings"
Poets and Dreamers: "on a farm in brownsville," "naomi," "only the ocotillo"
San Antonio Express News: "i want to wander"
Texas Poetry Calendar: "maximillians," "on the lawn".
Tupelo Press 3030: "birds again," "surrender"
Voice de la Luna: "catchment system," "eucharist of sky," "heaven scent," "stubborn sky," "stones telling," "sunset"
Waco Wordfest Anthology 2022: "reverberation"
Windhover: "beyond belief," "circuit preachers"
words gone wild: "how to make mud pie"

contents

crossings

on the lawn	17
stubborn sky	18
crossing the cibolo	20
bird speak	23
three lauds	24
stones telling: specht's road	25
catchment system	27
family portraits	30
mama i want to tell you	32
heaven scent	37
how to make mud pie	39
maybe i can	43
mouth of madness	44
wildness withers	45

shapeshifted: flying

wildness reaching in	51
a few seconds of rest	53
spreading the veil	54
i want to wander	55
birdfeeder	56
birds again	60
letting october in	64
maximillians	67
past the wall	68
limestone blessings	70
past the wall ii	72
behind these weeds	73
holding ground	75
reverberation	76
ten thousand wings	77

eucharist of sky	79
washing my breakfast cup	82
circuit preachers	84
homilies of spring	85
beyond belief	86
surrender	87
call to prayer	91
vespers	92
the garden prays	94
shape a prayer	95
tongues of heaven	98
river tell them	100

witness

syntax of difference	105
on a farm in brownsville	109
naomi	111
only the ocotillo	114
rachmaninoff off key	115
sometimes it's not enough	120

crossings

Come to me,
Here beside the River.
Plant yourself beside the River.

—Maya Angelou, *On the Pulse of Morning*

on the lawn

—for lin

he paces a mindful meditation
morning by morning he waters and
soothes the wound of this transplanted turf
surgically removed from the soil of its seed and
grafted onto this backyard body—
a recent victim of south texas scorch

his barefoot caresses—a shiatsu massage he hopes will
ease the ache of this new green skin
he wills to heal
blade by bermuda blade

stubborn sky

field full
of bull nettle   & cactus
—impassable   pasture

cattle ramble
chew cud

mud they've rolled in
stuck to their hides

caked and dried
to keep the biting
flies   at bay

~

if not for the rancher
his bale of hay

salt lick
well

these beasts would
not survive this
forbidding land

~

today   they hang out
at the tank   soak
knee-deep in what's left
of the water

wait for rain

~

don't even look up
this stubborn sky
isn't making   any

promises

crossing the cibolo

Texas springs were described . . . by early Texans as water which bursts from the plains, pure water rushing from rocks. . . . [Of the documented] two-hundred and eighty-one major springs in Texas, sixty-three no longer have enough flow to measure.

—*Texas Water Resources Institute,* Dec. 1980, Vol. 6 #10

cornsack   skitters
across this country road
—litter left to wander

vultures   peck at death
—road crew   cleaning up

silence   thick enough
to spread

~

i am driving into town
as we say   those of us
who live north of the cibolo

a day trip   for lunch with a friend

just passed the low water crossing
heading south—the first traffic light
for miles   signals

progress

here   they clear
building dreams

concrete sections of road
thunk under my tires as i ride

& at these four corners
the usual retail:

pharmacy
nail salon
fast food
bank

~

two chairs on an apartment
patio face this four-lane road

who sits here thinking:
    what a view

rooftops   populate the hills
where oaks once stood
each one an identical box

—eyesores
of uniformity

but for the beat nicks
& demon-weed

we'd all go down in
in this civilized ship

~

going back
traffic is stacked
nose to toes

& my body aches
in the waiting

—craving home

i'm city sick
my son used to say

   ~

nearing home:

a lone chestnut nibbles
at his bucket
flips his tail at the flies

   sky   hangs her heavy head
—gray clouds hug the horizon

   ~

in the distance
white   one steeple
needles the oaks

crossing the cibolo
dry stones echo
    the memory of water

bird speak

i feel better about the birds now
—their hunger   pressing

having paused my bean and chip
no cheese lunch   to feed them

after the finch came to the window
her red beak open   —bird speak
for thirst   the bath having gone

dry in a day   the way things do
in drought   not a drop
for days   for weeks now

~

but we humans   far from our roots:

open the tap   pop the top
of a single use bottle

—no reason to walk for water
—no need to draw it up from a well

no reason to visit the river: our guadalupe
only inches of it left   in places

our guadalupe: *mother of god*

pray for us now and
at the hour of our death

three lauds

—after Kimberly Johnson

1.

praise to the cypress
long legged beauty
kneeling on the banks of the guadalupe

2.

praise   oh! praise this shimmering
summer rain—withholding witness
tantric surge
orgasmic surprise

3.

praise this patient dry creek
—a woman   waiting
her wide   white limestone belly
swelling   water rushing through
her birth canal: life-giving

stones telling: specht's road

vulture   caracaras
atop hackberry trees

lining   this texas backroad

the creek runs dry —the sky
drizzling for days—
hasn't quenched her thirst

these curves   wind and dip
through low water crossings
full of stones   telling

~

here   where only stones remain
the cross that marked   his passing

—gone

i think about a man i knew
who drove home drunk

they begged him not to go
but he had to get home

in the darkness he didn't see
the curve   the dark water
    swirling

they found him   flooded in
    —his car   submerged

~

at the dogleg   just passed
the restaurant everybody loves

a black angus bull lying down
watches me pass   his pasture

he studies me   & the quarry
that piles across the road:

limestone
caliche
soil

the restauranteur fought
the quarry

speaking for the bull
& and the rest of us who breathe

but here it sits:

stirring up dust
spitting out mud

stripping every inch
of grace from the land's

face

puking   profit

onto the road

catchment system

thoughts dangle

hang

from the eaves

need

untangling

these:
stacked in corners
in cabinets
on pages
on shelves

—a life
in leaflets

what to do
with what doesn't'

have place

~

that transistor radio
we keep in the drawer
in case of nuclear war

—all those batteries

a glossy ad
for gutters

we've never had

    ~

thirty years
—the gush

ducked under
gallons   pouring

off the eaves

water

we could have

saved

but didn't

    ~

we needed:

designer lincoln
sprinkler system
st. augustine

green

granite countertops
slate floors
swimming pool

a catchment system
that never happened

or did it

~

when batteries die
transistors desist

perhaps:

merciful sky

we'll shower
under the gush

mouths   wide open

drinking
while we can

family portraits

white clouds accumulate   crowd
this summer sky—serenity speaking

a cow and her calf graze the field
—grown high with a thousand
   magnus cone flowers blooming
   painting   the pasture purple

two buck in velvet   laze and chew
pass the days   watching
the doe—her fawn newborn
      her surrogate   attending

agarita berries ripen in the sun
and she thinks about the time
daddy took the family dove hunting

how she and mama waited in the car
how he slung his gun over his shoulder
and climbed the fence to the sun-filled pasture
full of maize   how she could read the fence-post sign:

no trespassing

how she felt it then
said it aloud:

i hate him

how one day this same sun would stain her
white child's face with a galaxy of brown stars
how she'd spend money to remove those spots
spots she'd stare down in the bathroom mirror
the mirror that would never say what she wanted it to say
because those spots weren't going away
how she thinks she looks   just like her mother now
                         —especially her blue-lined hands

how she accidentally slammed her mother's hand
in the car door that hunting day   how her father
shoved her mother's hand in the icy water
and held it there no matter how
her mother squirmed and cried
how much she knew that hurt
how many times she said:

i'm sorry

i'm sorry mama

mama   i want to tell you

i stop
& nod

to the cement-truck
driver   crossing

the farm to market
road   —huge tumbler

   rolling

i think   about
ingredients:

shells
shale

limestone

too much
or
too little

causes

—disintegration

how many roads
we've travelled

    ~

the day   you
announced:

i've joined the army

how i thought
this   might

harden   you

how it did:

pills for rage
pills for sleep
pills for pain

~

too much

     for years

you wouldn't
look up

your back
to every wall

~

have you   ever

prayed

for rain
for a job

for a soul

~

today   you call

full
overflow

of the old   you
the one   i knew

mama

*i want
to tell you*

*i have
so many
ideas*

~

i think   about
intersections:

of faith
of mistakes

how i
came to
call you

my son

by making one

    ~

i think   about

the time   you
& i   prayed

    for our lives

—perpendicular
  roads

in front of
the cement plant

that day
the tornado

turned up
trucks

only yards
from us

    ~

how we shook
how the deluge

(almost) overtook

how we bow

to a god
neither of us

understands

heaven scent

—after Carl Sandburg

i love the scent
of a summer rain

—feline   marking its field

svelte swipe
through tall grass
resplendent bloom

liquid body

coming to cool
this feverish land

how we need this
quenching   now

—profuse perfume
   fresh from heaven

—a guest   surprising
   dropping in

   ~

she is the one you have adored
since your beginning

how she nurtured you
cultivated every root

her gentle touch   enough

to coax even the most
stubborn seed from its pod

& in her puddling remains

    diamonds   glisten

    children   dance

how to make mud pie

*i don't live
in a neighborhood Ms.*
he says   insisting

*nothing happens
on my street*

this thick   city
boy: uniformed/scrubbed/polished
& sent to school

his black hair   stiffened
stands at attention

his head   is hurting (i am sure)
from too much   sitting still

i lean into his round face
—willing words
his imagination—a phantom—

~

*how many   of you
have ever made mud pies*

a few hands   rise
—confessing actual play

outside

go home   i say
turn on the hose

make mud

they giggle

~

my toes   flex their memory
stretch their   crooked necks
& i am standing   knee deep
in rainwater

the sky is wiping its eyes
dim thunder   rumbling

we   have all flown outside
waving—squawking birds
converging   on a makeshift lake
at the corner of collier drive and vilbig

water   runs to greet us like an old friend
white feet slap the street and we   wade in

~

a few fat drops hit   shower us wet
—cold   clothes cling   barefoot toes

stomp splash—child song in the street

—rain dance
—glee club

goose bumps

~

i squat   squish mud
between my toes
shovel up a clump of oozing earth

fling it
at the first unsuspecting
one of us

a burst of laughter—splat—
a flinched face—splat—
an arched back   *i got you!*

we are merciless
    warriors   taking aim

duck/dive/slip/slide

run from each other
like we   might really
die

in seconds: an hour passes

~

my breath comes fast
i am full of fun & covered

in baking clay

i lie down in the gutter
on long   green grass
bent   under
this sudden stream

fresh water
wash   me clean

maybe i can

> *Eight million metric tons of plastic are dumped into the oceans each year . . . the equivalent of nearly 57,000 blue whales. By 2050, ocean plastic will outweigh all the ocean's fish.*
>
> —conservation.org

a balcony of ears listens but does not hear
silently   the sea becomes a rank bloom
& destiny unwinds   wanting gravity

what did you say   did i say it too

i trusted you   yet under every word—dark nonsense
—cowardice retching like the guilty
what kind of rulers are we
should we throw virgins into the fire

earth yearns   eons crack open
i tell you   i tell you   now
(as if i could   maybe i can)
with the sea as my witness:

every sip and zip
every single-use toss
every cling-wrapped glass
every sea-turtle trapped

every brain undone
every giant garbage patch
every deadly red tide
every entangled whale

i tell you   i tell you now

i take it all   i take it all
back

mouth of madness

> *Behold, consider, we are all thy people . . . holy cities . . . a wilderness . . . Zion . . . a wilderness, Jerusalem a desolation.*
> —Isaiah 64:9–10

today rain   scrub jay bathes
—the redbud   her boudoir

gyration of delight   & dust
overruling yesterday's anvil of heat

grace: this earth turns
        leans
        yearns for change

her huge   face —a painted grey shadow
has closed her eyes   to this:

ancient   reign of fire   of blood
mouth of madness   overflowing

stop

we all   drink from this fountain
circling earth: holy holy holy

water

how
can this
be so

wildness withers

The United States' President Donald Trump signed thirty-seven executive orders in the first hundred days of his presidency. One of them ordered the Secretary of the Interior to find ways to allow drilling for oil in national parks.

under   unconscious

weight

—greedy pen

thoughtless

power

worm

unearthing

~

oval   omnipotence

sits   silk-suited

sign
sign

sign of indifference

never mind *the fall*
never mind Atlantis

sunk under

save

nothing
nothing

at all

shapeshifted: flying

*. . . we must walk out under the open sky
and let the beauty we encounter break our hearts
and break us open to the work we are each called to do . . .*

—Wendy Sarno, *Rebearths*

wildness   reaching in

just now   the wren
flew in   —my studio

door: flung open wide

she perched
her perkiness

a moment

i spoke
she nodded

& hopped
along the rail

& onto the shelf
making her dainty

self   at home

~

i wonder:

*is this the same
familiar one who nested
on my porch this spring*

the one we witnessed
    day by day

—she and her mate—

    build their nest
    tend their eggs
    feed three

upturned yellow beaks
worm by worm

   ~

oh   what tender love
nature makes

how close she comes
—wildness   reaching in

as if   to lift our chins

   ~

i ask you:

*what more
could you*

need

a few seconds of rest

as i sit counting they fly
—one hundred and seventeen
in this one half of an hour

it is number sixty-three
who stops to rest
—a snout-nosed silhouette
　　above my head

i can see her shadow
through the thin taupe umbrella:

her wings unfolding
her two antennae
the tell-tale nose

she follows
after summer rains

i suppose she's stopped
to catch her breath
but in her few seconds of rest

she has taken mine　　　away

spreading the veil

mockingbird sings his song
—a long road of quick curves

redbud blooms her profuse magenta
—a wild abandon

wren nests   makes of her work
— a moving meditation

bright yellow wings light the field
—flight in oaky shadows

arugula bolts from its bed
—fingers spreading the veil

& i am plumped and feathered
    in still   small spaces

my mouth   remembering

—the quick curve

—wild abandon

i want to wander

down

this oak-lined
road

not knowing
where

but   watching

~

caliche   under my feet
red-headed beak

knocking
—& nothing

~

imprint of time

each step
and the next

blooming:

huisache
red bud
lilac

skull

birdfeeder

long   the hawk   perches
—a finial atop the deck-post in my   backyard

        stillness   hunting

only his head turns   keen eyes   unblinking

this bird of prey   waits:
    for the lizard to slip   from its   burrow
    for the grass-snake   slithering

his red breast   his hunger
pressed   against grey   sky

~

i think   of you: my mind   returning
to east texas pines
to walks through loblolly   stands

i loved to hold   your grandfather   hands

the middle finger of your left one   —a nub—
a nub you cut off with an axe   accidentally
as a boy   chopping wood

how i wondered about that finger
its smooth   round end
how you said: *it doesn't*   *hurt*
anymore

me: listening
learning   about wounds   & healing
how a person   can live on
even   with some parts   —severed

   ~

tiny   & white   i was thin   *like a bird*
mama said   my mouth always   open

wanting   my hunger   pressing

   ~

in your backyard i was your little   bird
   & you   were my   feeder

me   helping you:

~place the cypress knees   you
  hollowed out   stuffed
   with lard & seed

~remove the blue-martin nest
  from atop its pole   high above   us

lower it down like this
clean it out   each spring

you said   we were bird   housekeeping

~ turn the worms—squirming
  squirming mass   feeding them   scraps
  digging my bony fingers
  into the porcelain bath you   salvaged
  —a tub you buried
& filled with mud

   —*food*   you said   *for the birds*
                                     for the fish
                                     good   for the soil

& in the woods: your *caw*   *ca-caw*
calling the crow *shhh*   *listen*
you said bending low   *hear that:*

                                       bird song

   ~

at eighty-one
you danced your last   jig
—irish blood   becoming   soil

me   standing beside
your hospital bed

life is good
you said

   ~

today   i am   bird

housekeeping

i place bird houses
in my own backyard—material   bits

threads for   nesting

the wren sings
& i feed her   hunger   pressing

       ~

i am like you   bird feeder

parts of me   —severed—
now rounding out   —becoming

painless   smooth   nubs

birds   again

this time—the wren
          —i think

has flown in—snagged
a feather for her nest

from the found object bouquet
on the desk that sits   ~askew

wasp nests
ball moss
lime-green
lichened sticks

bones bleached
     & stones

     ~

a flurry of dust on the desk: a clue

our doors are flung open
—screenless to every cerulean sky
we welcome whatever comes

once (and i am certain of this) raccoon
came in   her paws—tiny fingers
white   ghostlike   mono-printed
the mirrored glass on the wall

she must have stood in the chair
sitting there did she stare
at her reflection   did she think
she had found true love

or   did she run from this unknown

~

have you ever seen them play
fat   families under the full
moon   frolicking up   from the field
for easy food   they steal

~

the last time i left town
hubby   not wanting to answer
the cat's demands:

now now now   in   out
around the house he goes
because he knows there is
another   tom—a stray
who thinks he's found
a home   but no

not if my cat
has his say

~

so   hubby left the den
(half-garage-half-den
half-claimed by the cat
half-claimed by him)

door

(yes   you guessed)

open

    ~

this time: skunk
thought well of the invitation
decided to make herself at home
behind the shelves of games and toys

when hubby returned to the open den
from underneath   he heard the noise

a puppy's nose   a yip   a yap
& that skunk stunk like a cold hard slap

    ~

hours later i got the call
skunk had soundly stunk

them all:

puppy/hubby/yoga mat
lawn chairs/luggage/coats
& hats/carpet/lounger

all thrown out

peroxide/bleach/soda/soap
he had scrubbed
there was   no

hope

    ~

you say:
now you close the door

i say:
no   there will be more

letting october in

> ... *Entomologists . . . [say] yellow jackets are fascinating insects, with all the sophistication of behavior found in bees, ants and other elaborately social insects . . . not preprogrammed automatons, but [that they] learn from experience, . . . communicate with one another, conveying their intentions, work assignments, the location of a hot new outdoor restaurant.*
> —The New York Times, August 1999

you know you're an empath
when yellow jackets swarm
the hummingbird feeder for sugar-water
and long after the hummingbirds no longer come
you scrub the feeder   hang it back outside
~for the yellow jackets

& when your husband says:

look at all those bees   meaning:

*danger   danger
i should kill them*

you say:

*those are yellow jackets
leave them alone
they're hungry*

when a few of them fly inside
because you've flung
the door open wide
~letting october in

& some of them get stuck   behind the kitchen glass
—can't find their way back outside

you pick one of your grandmother's china cup-saucers
from the cabinet   fill it with a tablespoon of sugar water
    set it on the sill

then   you close the door
to keep more yellow jackets
from finding their way inside

you catch the ones you can with a tissue
—fling them out the door

back to their freedom

        ~

thinking: *they're all safe now*
you sit down to breakfast

but as you take that bite
of almond bread and avocado
    a tiny movement
    catches your eye

it's one last yellow jacket
climbing up and down
the door jamb   round
and round the handle

like he knows:
this is the way out

but the door is closed
so   you get up
and open it

& when he flies   outside

—in an instant
you   are shape-shifted:

flying
with him

into the autumn air

maximillians

wildflowers rise
from the side of the road
into the autumn air

yellow faces wave in the breeze
hands   raised high in praise

—street preachers
   of faith
   in seasons

a bright reminder
of how persistence pays

jubilant crowds
of perennial joy

—life outdoing itself
year   after year

native texans
—tenacious to the core

growing   straight up
out of these
limestone
walls

past the wall

black grackles fly
from scrub oaks that lean
like cowpokes
after a long hard ride

in the garden we manicure   to pretend dominion
over seedlings   crab grass—the power of earth

we've tamed most of an acre
with water—dug under and computerized

drought tolerant sod
sandy soil
xeriscape: feathergrass   skull-cap   sage

we think: *this is beautiful*

we spend hours a week grooming
the prolific hair of this imported landscape
and more   tugging at stubborn errant growth

~

i wander past the wall we stacked
with a thousand limestones—the old ones
who first claimed this ancient land

remember: how small i really am

stand hip-high in maximillian sprouts
that from flat-dead last december
will reach ten feet tall by fall
—produce myriad yellow faces—feed bees

i wade in the violet wake
of wild petunias and the
viridian lace of prairie coneflower

i rest under the gracious
shade of the prairie flameleaf
we call simply: sumac—native texan
whose leaves flame bright
cadmium orange come fall

stunning us all every year

this tree   and all its native kin
    —given half-a-chance

will overgrow   easily
    overcome
       this very   path

limestone blessings

i found three stones
—some might say: ordinary
like my mother-in-law did
when I reveled in the wild yellow
of coreopsis and verbena sweet that
grow because they want more than god
to live in the hill country heat,

oh   you mean the weeds   she said

i flinched at the blow of her disdain
(*never cast pearls before swine*)

the first stone lay patiently in its place
(it had spoken to me yesterday as i passed
but i had let it lie) so today   at its insistence
i bent to gather its wisdom (i collect this wherever
i find it)   placed the forefinger of my right hand
in the groove it offered me for that perfect purpose
felt the full   cool cradle of its company

one step left   humming a subtle pink
sat the second stone   her heart-shape
leaned easy as sleep on the creek bed edge
—invited me to carry her home (these rocks
like found fossils   are strong medicine)

then   i left the pebbled gully
that i step over every day
holding its limestone blessings

this time   walked along the familiar trail
intent on going home   like a child with a wild
bouquet   when i stepped the payne's gray stairs
of stone   left by some earthly urge to shift
its weight   the place I stop to see sunset
or inhale silence as I sit   i heard the third
—an oval lobe with an ochre tone
smooth and not quite flat like an animal's ear

but i left it there   listened instead to the
voice of years   for seven steps
i heard the noise:

be still
settle down
loudmouth
grow up

but some vibration shook the sound

and i returned
to claim the third

past the wall ii

red grass rides
on winter waves
bends and bows
allows this open mouth
some graceful space
some sacred place

some secret speaks
its mind behind
these rustling weeds
these pubic curls
this wanton wailing
reach

behind these weeds

barefooted   i sit   —grounding
in front of me
earth   has adorned her head

red tallow leaf
thin yellow rim
in a sunlit spot

mockingbird feather
—white-tipped flag
waves in green grass blades

she speaks her medicine:

*your sacred song
is always with you*

*make your own
true sound*

    ~

lattice of light
and shadow   the oak
throws her arms open

a branch   a bridge
drawing my eyes
upward   always upward

golden pecan
red oak   red
yellow elm

—last leaves

the wisdom of trees:

let go
pull in

center
ground

wait   for sun

holding ground

> *[When the limbs of trees] melt into one another, their bark conjoining into a single continuous skin, their vascular systems growing and uniting [scientists call this] "tree snogging" . . . [technically called] "inosculation," from the Latin* osculare, *meaning "to kiss." It can happen across trees and between species too.*
> —Robert Macfarlane, *Underland*

the oak moths have come in clouds
just in time for the cedar wax wings to feast
on them   these birds perched at the top of my tallow

i watch them fly out a few feet
catch a bug mid-air   swallow him whole
they dive and swerve   swerve and dive
return to perch on the same bare branch

this tallow i planted from a seedling
i found one spring   pushing up amid
the periwinkles—solo   so lonely
it looked to be   so tenderly i dug it up

plucking it from its birthplace   placing
it mid-yard   surrounding it with stones
—a circumference of care
—a beware sign
so hubby would not mow my seedling child down

this tree   considered trash by many here
has grown taller than our roof
has shaded my napping head
me lying on grandmother's quilt

me and the tree—snogging
sharing skin
sharing blood

—each holding
the other   to earth

reverberation

There is in all visible things a hidden wholeness.
—Thomas Merton

blooms bend their heads
to earth   turning

melancholy moon
makes her waning

question after question
tills the soil

—smell of matter   rotting
this humus   becoming

~

yellow stalks rise from stone
purple spires   point upward

always upward   how the sky
becomes a highway now

birds reverberating the ancient ways
widening vee   eternal swirl

swath of flight and bellow
below: the resting pinion

—evergreen

ten thousand wings

> *As many as one million raptors & over thirty species have been counted passing through the Texas Coastal Bend area on their annual fall migration south.*
> —Hawk Watch International

—this   hawk flock
flies   south

over   my house

on an invisible path
only   the old ones know

this ancient wisdom:

*go before the north
takes hold*

~

i stop   mid-street
   mouth agape

looking up

this glide
—at least forty feet

wide

marking its place
in october's sky

~

in my life
i have not seen
this   nor maybe

will i ever   again

   ~

hush

the portal

opens

eucharist of sky

Unprecedented severe cold & a foot of snow in Michocan, Mexico freezes one-and-a-half million Monarch butterflies.
—March 12, 2016

if

i had attended
the workshop

i would
have missed

this:

visitation

of cranes

~

the way
they sing

this religion
of birds

eucharist
of sky

how this raven

black

harbinger

calls

~

these billowing
clouds are mouths

here
the earth
—fuchsia skirt

whirling   feet
bare   &
pounding

there

—a potter
throwing clay:

wild

discontent

~

this   is not
democracy

dictators
rage

monarchs
die

~

remove
these rulers

none   of them

tell   the

truth

washing my breakfast cup

at the sink   i sponge lipstick
lip prints from its clear rim

warm water and soap
soothing my skin

~i gaze   out the kitchen window

admiring the plants i've potted
on the porch:

periwinkle
bougainvillea
rosemary
sage

~

consider seasons:

    how soon these blooms will fade

but before nostalgia overtakes
    monarch   perches

upon the petal of the sage
—orange & black   stained glass

~

she folds
unfolds
folds again

bow and dip
bow and dip

i cannot help myself

i stop   watch
    —called to worship

by wings

circuit preachers

praise to the cranes that vee this march sky
how they mingle and float a moment as if to
confer   then converge
—revisit form

i eavesdrop   their playful conversation
—tinkling glass
on an elegant azure table

how do they know the north so well

it seems they have convened here
—circuit preachers
   passing through
to bless the forgiven

i toast their returning with tears
like baptismal waters
with these   winter-weary eyes

homilies of spring

priestess robed in cool gray
bends her sky back
leans morning over

drips baptism   with kiss
upon misty kiss   from fingertips
long and lean

enchanted wings sing
—salvation's song

purple petals pray
grass kneels   wild and white
with winter dry   receives communion

soil

feathers float   fall like   grace

through incense of mint
and sage   as age
upon age believes
the cadmium whisper

the spoken hope of geranium bloom
the branches dancing liturgy

the homilies of spring

beyond belief

sparrow soprano sings for seed
from the cyclone   while i think
about sunday mornings

about how *this* morning
i have what i was looking for
during all those years:

dressing in hose and heels
dragging children choking
on bow ties and starch
to squirm on polished pews
—sleep through

priestly profundity
anxious to shed their shoes
show *me* how to worship

barefoot

how to robe myself like the monarch
—float from flower to flower

lift on light air
up and out   away

beyond belief   into

        being

surrender

It took me a long time to learn I could survive as flame.
        —Kyndall Rae Rothaus

today

is the friday
some   call

good

i   would not

given
reported

events
nevertheless

i am fasting

    ~

(this   is not

what you

    think)

this   is not

me   being religious:

fish for food
not eating chocolate

tying myself
in knots

not me kneeling

obligatory

mass
misunderstanding

this   is not
confession:

[father
forgive me
for i have
sinned]

    ~

if sin
is losing   all

direction

not following
the thorny path

calling in guides

—unseen
    feathered heads
    red-breasted

    & howling

if   not knowing
or
denial
or
cursing

burns me up

—i   am flame

    ~

bowing   to the

poppy's face

crimson
sunning

this quilt
each stitch

hand sewn

the elm—

how she
    leafs out

three
hundred
times

this
sign

~

if not

dry   white
grass

galaxies

spinning

    a fontanelle

then   i surrender
        this skin:

five

million

tiny

hairs

call to prayer

scissor-tailed kingbird
takes her place on a wire

faces eastern sky

vespers

pastures   slathered
in mustard yellow

—huisache in bloom

the roadside   a reverie:

paintbrush
bluebonnet
cosmos

cacophony of color

~

lone hawk
perched on a post

keeping watch

burrow   brown & spotted
buries his nose
in new growth

flags flap in the wind

a palomino   grazing:

soft curve
of her jaw

nuzzles   nips
the earth

receiving

~

i want   this
kind of trust

i want   this
kind of gratitude

i want my body
to open & seed

like this:

wild
flower

~

& when evening comes
—the turning earth

primrose opens
her yellow face

in praise of the day

i want   to pray

like this

the garden prays

i will sing like the frog from the lily pad
lying in the light of the full white moon

i will throat each melodious note
into the auspicious air

i will send scent like the pinch of mint
i touch to my tingling tongue

i will bury the ache of your heavy heart
like the garden shard   hide it deep in the dark

i will feed you   full on nectar's sweet
—wash your feet in the forest stream

i will lay on hands like the dragonfly lands
let spirit speak   clear as her transparent wing

shape   a prayer

fingertips touch
moist   black earth

i pluck a piece
of purple heart

& think of you

bare legs
like mine   as white

as the gardenias
you loved

~

the two of us

in short pants
for the first time

each spring

mother & daughter
weeding st. augustine

~

tugging
tenacious strands
from the front flower bed

or so you called it

though there were
rarely   flowers there

only two
ligustrums grew

arching over
the picture window

this window—
our winter perch

the two of us:

naming birds
claiming spring

wondering

~

your voice: a giggle

come quick
jack frost was here

my gleeful feet
—bare ice

under your
generous hips

your breath
—warm

against my head

whispering:

when the robins come
it will be spring

ligustrums listening
laden   blue

berries—their grape-like

shape   a prayer

this moment:

    suspended

tongues of heaven

at this meadow's edge
—plowed & turned under—
i sit   seeding myself

sod   willing my feet to root

i wait at the cave   at this mouth
of limestone   with cypress kneeling
in silence we share   like this water

leaning against cypress breast
my eyes follow one leaf   as it floats
so we both float   on the pulse of river

how many mouths have drunk here
how many hours have passed
—this water   watching

    ~

long   curve of sky
march of cranes
redbud shadow — spent magenta

comfort of skin

if this is my last life

how these eyes will miss:

the consort of bees
—hum of hundreds—
under the huisache

the body's pulse
the thrum of earth
under my back

how   these hills put on
their verbena robe
how the breasted bird
wears her crimson amulet

how   the cypress weeps
over the guadalupe
sweep of moss & swallow

—this shoulder of silence
silence we share   like water

not calculations (things
never add up) but this

river:

carrying on
holding green
sway   over
these stones

~ language

of trees   each
branch   curve & curl

—tongues   of heaven

river   tell them

loon silks her song—a scarf
suspended in evening air

raindrops orgasm   languish
fall   from philodendron tips

river greens its way along   winding
slow like a grinding stone

—slow   the way time goes
   at the end

witness

. . . surely what might save us as we move forwards into the precarious, unsettled centuries ahead is collaboration: mutualism, symbiosis, the inclusive human work of collective decision-making extended to more-than-human communities.

—Robert Macfarlane, *Underland*

syntax of difference

i have read   that
   covering my head

with white   will hold precious
life-force   in   keep

negativity   out

~

in the parking lot
of the grocery store

i wrap my head

in a simple scarf
white   turban style

my pulse quickens

[some
have died
  for less]

~

here   a motorcycle
waits for its patriot

his flags   flying
his choice made clear
in print:

america is a christian nation

(i pray he isn't packing
his values in his sleeve)

    ~

entering:

cool   din
bar codes scan
bodies stand

concrete floor
crushing spines

    ~

young woman
baby on board

stops   steps back

what is this

    reverence
    fear

no matter   i feel it

[difference]

    ~

no one   speaks
no eyes   meet mine

(save the babies
—they can see)

    ~

in the aisle
i pass a man

wrinkled brow   staring
he sits on his parked cart

motor running:

can't find something
i say

chicken broth: swanson's
i've got a very sick wife

i'll find it for you
i say

& we   are

one

train   of two
on the move

    ~

what's your name
he wants to know

i want to know:

what   is a name

immigrant
citizen

muslim
catholic
jew

syntax
of difference

on a farm in brownsville

Here at our sea-washed, sunset gates shall stand
A mighty woman with a torch, whose flame
Is the imprisoned lightning, and her name
Mother of Exiles.
—Emma Lazarus, *The New Colossus*

rust-colored steel
cuts through

melon & mesquite

chops this land in half

where hundred year-old oaks
were felled   in the weld

security   unsecured

from this landowner's porch:

no more pastoral view
no more free passage
from pasture to pasture

where he and his father
and his father before him

who came: chasing the dream

grew cotton and corn
sorghum and cane

for a hundred years
& more

now   this farmer
            who feeds us

must ask   permission
to pass   from one piece
of his own land   to another

naomi

along the rio grande
among carnelian melons
& orange   groves

you can hear the coyotes
crooning   to a moon
wide and bright   as

the river   she loves

naomi crossed this borderland
for freedom   cradling her infant
son in her arms   smothering his cries

to quiet him:

she cupped   his mouth
with her warm   brown hand

~

she comes each week   to clean

solo hablo un poquito español
i speak only a little spanish   i say

she speaks no english   and so we agree
to teach each other   laughing a lot
at the language

barrier

~

we are standing in the kitchen
with her naked toddler son   the one
she cradled and silenced in the box car
where the coyotaje had hidden them

the one she rode from her
beloved guatemala to tejas

        so many hours

con muchas otras desplazadas
          so many displaced

~

& when the rocking
of the hot   hot box
      did not stop
her son's crying

i had to cover his mouth with my hands

she says

and just at this
her son   has to go
& does not know

he does not know
how his mother's hands
have just cleaned this tile
how she has scrubbed

& cupped   to save him

and so he lets his urine:

an easy   yellow flow
on the floor   but quick

his mother cups her hands
     to catch it . . .

only the ocotillo

they rode in silence

silence

across the great river

silence

across the canyons

silence   wide open

splitting

seeds   of so many

each   last breath

echoing

 this valley

receiving last rights

from the sighing night

—only the ocotillo

as witness

rachmaninoff   off key

a minister
maybe   a member

of the house of restoration
this man   stands

in the street
asking   for handouts
&
my hand's out
the window

holding   spare change

~

coming toward me

—his steps   tentative
—his eyes   locked on mine

he stops

a few feet from me
takes a tiny bow

~

emboldened by this:

act of prayer
he approaches

holding a pamphlet
in his large   dark

hand   he hands

me the slip

for the son of man
has come to seek
and to save that
which was lost
it says

    ~

this man's story
i do not know

but i   have seen
his eyes   in my mirror

drunk
punctured

flatness   looking back

—song birds   soaked
   in oil

    ~

perhaps like saul   like me

(persecutor
persecuted)

his name has changed
& now   a witness

he wears   fluorescent-yellow
—vestments—city-issued

that make
his claim

to this intersection:

—of failure
  and faith

legal

   ~

you say
god helps those
who help themselves

and my hand
out the window

will only encourage
his begging

i say

there comes   a blackness

consuming

when flesh   abandons bones
when confounding voices

deafen reason

when every hand
on every clock

turns back
to the hour

of your regret

& the whiskey
you loved

stings
—nettle in your blood

regret   ballooning
in your veins

as you needle
through   one more

hour

like rachmaninoff   off key

and you cannot stop

you cannot   stop
you   cannot stop

~

*and you feel
your body*

*crawling
crawling*

to its end

*begging
begging*

to be

blinded

by

the light

sometimes   it's not enough

> *Since 1970, the average global temperature has risen by 0.9°. . . . This additional heat has increased the chances for severe heat waves, drought, and other forms of extreme weather.*
> —*National Geographic News,* August 21, 2012

snuggled under a throw
in the corner of my studio
i watch yesterday's snow:

wet clumps   slip
from umber branches

if it can snow   in south texas
anything can happen

    ~

in california
neighborhoods burn

today

from outside the wall
of wildfire flames
you call:

pray for me/pray for my home/pray
for those whose homes are burning now

you say

anything can happen

    ~

like this marriage
made of relentless persistence
of lusty pillars turned to dust
of jealous misapprehension
of leaving and leaving again

of not knowing   what it takes
to come home   to crazy

how much   holding on
matters   & no matter
how you hold on   sometimes

it's not enough

~

like the time the tornado in dallas
tore the newborn
right out   of his father's arms

how i cried   for days and days

and days

how i prayed:
    for that baby
    for the father

who could not   hold him

anything   can happen

~

like the time the waters rose in houston

after the hurricane
how those johnny-boats on trailers
headed down the road

to the rescue

   ~

if only

that's all it took
—a bunch of cowboys
  in pick-ups

& courage

About the Author

d. ellis phelps' poems, essays, and visual art have appeared widely online and in print. As an educator, she has taught fine arts in various venues with students of all ages for decades.

She has edited more than a dozen anthologies and is the author of three books of poetry: *what she holds* (Moon Shadow Sanctuary Press, 2020), *what holds her* (Main Street Rag, 2019), and *words gone wild* (Kelsay Books, 2021); and of the novel, *Making Room for George* (MSSP, 2016). She writes and publishes the work of other writers and artists on her blog *formidable woman sanctuary*. She is founding and managing editor of Moon Shadow Sanctuary Press and of *fws: international journal of literature & art*.

www.ingramcontent.com/pod-product-compliance
Lightning Source LLC
Chambersburg PA
CBHW022014160426
43197CB00007B/431